Fossil Ridge Public Library District
386 Kennedy Road
Braidwood, Illinois 60408

8/99

The Let's Talk Library™

Let's Talk About When Someone You Love Is in a Nursing Home

Diana Star Helmer

The Rosen Publishing Group's
PowerKids Press™
New York

Published in 1999 by The Rosen Publishing Group, Inc.
29 East 21st Street, New York, NY 10010

First Edition

Book Design: Erin McKenna

Photo Illustrations: Cover and all photo illustrations by Seth Dinnerman.

Helmer, Diana Star, 1962–
    Let's talk about when someone you love is in a nursing home / by
Diana Star Helmer.
                p.   cm. — (Let's talk library)
    Includes index.
    Summary: Discusses why someone would enter a nursing home, what nursing homes
are like, and how to act when visiting someone there.
    ISBN 0-8239-5190-1
    1. Nursing homes—Juvenile literature. 2. Nursing home care—Juvenile literature.
3. Grandparent and child—Juvenile literature. [1. Nursing homes.] 1. Title. II. Series
RA997.H44
362.1'6—dc21   97–41241
                                                                          CIP
                                                                           AC

Manufactured in the United States of America

Table of Contents

Susan's Grandma

Susan answered the telephone. It was her favorite uncle. Uncle John asked to speak to Susan's mom. When Mom hung up, she said, "Grandma's in the hospital. She broke her hip."

Susan remembered having a broken arm. "Will Grandma be better soon?" she asked.

"Older people don't heal as quickly as kids do," Mom said. "Grandma will need lots of help for a while. She's going to move to a nursing home."

◀ Sometimes it's hard to hear that someone you know is moving to a nursing home.

What Is a Nursing Home?

A nursing home is a place where older people go to live when they are very sick or cannot take care of themselves anymore. Doctors, nurses, and **aides** (AYDZ) help people there. Some people in nursing homes are very sick. Others aren't so sick, but they're not very strong. They need help with things like cooking, eating, and taking **medicine** (MEH-dih-sin). A nursing home is a place where people care for others.

Aides work at nursing homes all day and through the night to help the people who live there. ▶

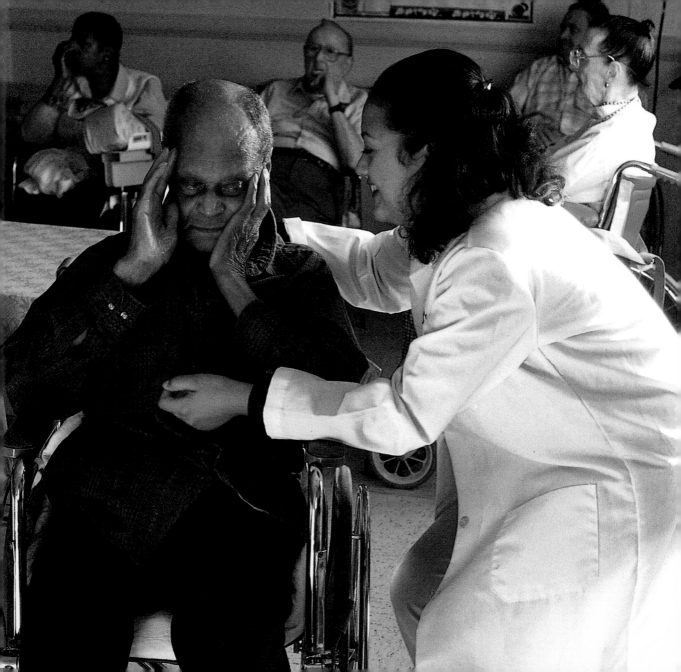

Nursing Homes Can Be Different

When someone you love goes to live in a nursing home, you will still be able to visit that person. You might miss going to Grandma's house. Her room in the nursing home may be too small for all of her things. The nursing home also might smell like cleaners or medicine. Nursing homes are cleaned often so **germs** (JERMZ) don't make people sick. Even nursing home food may smell differently than family cooking.

◄ You can help your grandparent or friend to feel better by bringing him something special.

Houses and Nursing Homes

You may think that your family can care for a sick person at your house. But there may not always be someone home to help, especially if you go to school or your parents work. A nurse or an aide is always there to help a person who needs it. Nursing homes have lots of helpers for their **residents** (REZ-ih-dents). They help sick people to sit down, stand up, walk, or take baths. Nursing homes have wide halls for **wheelchairs** (WEEL-chayrz) and elevators so residents won't fall on stairs.

Nurses take care of nursing home residents ▶
and help them to stay healthy.

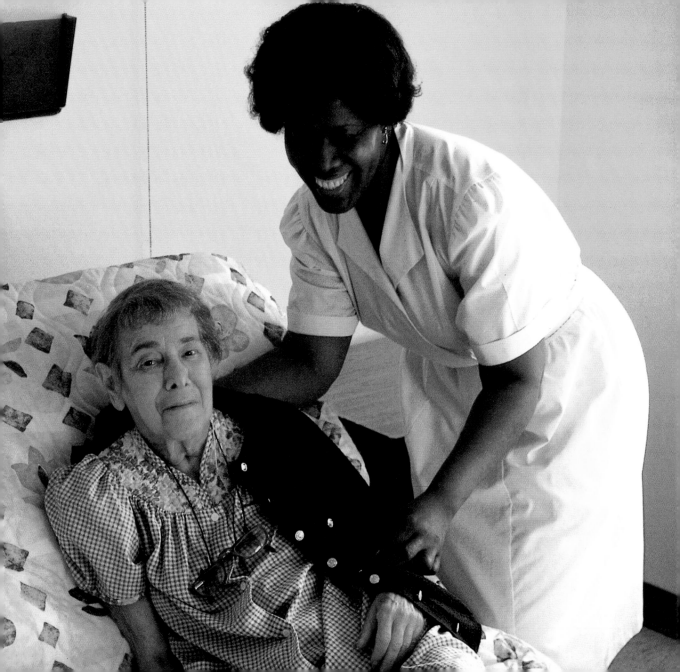

All Kinds of Help

Some people in nursing homes have bodies that aren't working as well as they once did. It's easy to tell when someone breaks a bone. But it's harder to know if a person has a **disease** (dih-ZEEZ). A disease is when someone's body stops working well because of a very bad illness.

Some diseases make it hard for a person's brain to work. These people need help remembering when to eat or rest, or what telephone numbers they might want to dial.

◀ Some older people stay in nursing homes when they are getting over an illness or injury.

13

Visiting

People who are not well may sometimes look and act different than healthy people. But no matter what kind of sickness a person has, he or she can still feel happy or sad, just like you.

Sometimes new places are scary. Even though a nursing home might feel different at first, your visit to a grandparent or friend in the nursing home will make that person feel good. Making that person happy will also make you happy.

Visiting your friend at the nursing home will ▶ remind her that you care about her.

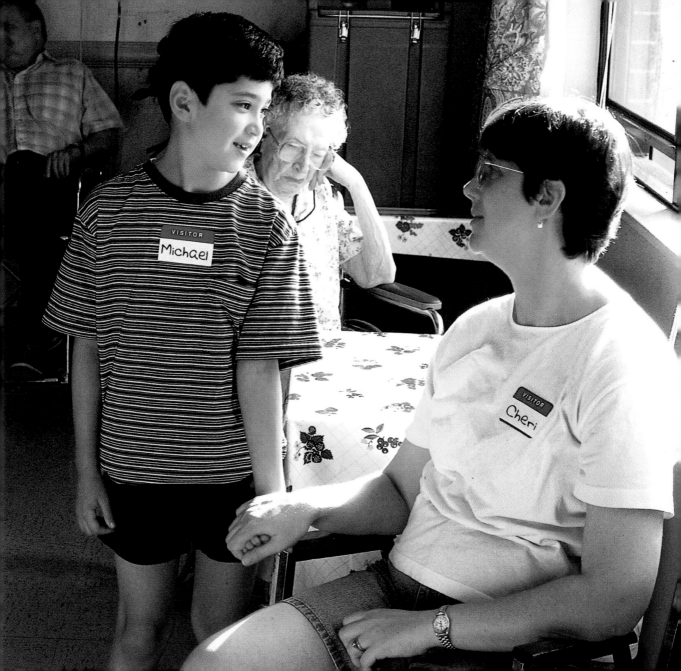

Changes

A nursing home is a good, safe place for someone you love. There will be new people to meet and new ways of doing things. Grandpa might have to share his bedroom with a roommate. Grandma might have to ride on a bus instead of driving her car. Your mom, dad, or grandparent might feel sad about these changes. They might show their worries by acting mad. But they aren't mad at you. They just need to get used to the new **situation** (sit-choo-AY-shun).

◄ Your grandparent can introduce you to
his new friends at the nursing home.

When You Visit

Even though a nursing home is a good place for people to live, residents might still miss seeing old friends while they are there. They'll miss talking and spending time together. Did you know that hugs make people feel better? When you visit the nursing home, ask if you can hug your grandma or friend. If she's tired, she might just like to sit and hold your hand. You can think of it as a very small hug!

Spending time with your grandparent ▶
will make both of you feel special.

Being Together

Spending time with you is the most important thing to your Grandma at the nursing home. You can read to Grandma, write a letter for her, do puzzles together, or ask her to tell you stories about your family.

Sometimes nursing home residents get together to sing or make crafts. You could meet Grandpa's new friends. You could go for a walk or give Grandpa a wheelchair ride!

◀ Helping your grandma even with everyday things can be fun.

Love Is the Best Medicine

It may be hard for someone you love to get used to living in a nursing home. Sometimes it's hard for your parents too. That's why families are so important. Even when things around you change, the love in your family stays the same. You can show your love with hugs and smiles, or by talking and listening. Showing love isn't always easy when you're worried about new things. But love makes people strong enough to get through the hard times.

Glossary

aide (AYD) A helper.

disease (dih-ZEEZ) A sickness.

germ (JERM) A tiny living thing that can cause sickness and infection.

medicine (MEH-dih-sin) Something that makes a sick person feel better.

resident (REZ-ih-dent) A person who stays in a nursing home.

situation (sit-choo-AY-shun) A problem; an event that happens.

wheelchair (WEEL-chayr) A chair on wheels used by people who are sick or unable to walk.

Index

A
aides, 6, 10

C
changes, 17

D
disease, 13
doctors, 6

E
elevators, 10

F
feelings, 14, 17, 18
food, 9

G
germs, 9

L
love, 22

M
medicine, 6, 9

N
nurses, 6, 10

R
residents, 10, 18, 21

S
sick, being, 6, 10, 13
situations, 17

T
talking, 18, 22
together, being, 18, 21

V
visiting, 14, 18, 21

W
wheelchairs, 10, 21